# Jobs if You Like...

# Math

Charlotte Guillain

Heinemann

**www.capstonepub.com**
Visit our website to find out more information about Heinemann-Raintree books.

**To order:**
☎ Phone 800-747-4992
💻 Visit www.capstonepub.com
to browse our catalog and order online.

© 2013 Heinemann Library
an imprint of Capstone Global Library, LLC
Chicago, Illinois

Edited by Rebecca Rissman, Daniel Nunn, and
  Adrian Vigliano
Designed by Steve Mead
Picture research by Elizabeth Alexander
Originated by Capstone Global Library
Printed and bound in China by South China Printing
  Company

16 15 14 13 12
10 9 8 7 6 5 4 3 2 1

**Library of Congress Cataloging-in-Publication Data**
Guillain, Charlotte.
  Math / Charlotte Guillain.—1st ed.
    p. cm.—(Jobs if you like...)
  Includes bibliographical references and index.
  ISBN 978-1-4329-6808-3 (hb)—ISBN 978-1-4329-6819-9
(pb)  1. Mathematics—Vocational guidance—Juvenile
literature. I. Title.
  QA10.5.G85 2013
  510.23—dc23                    2011031928

**Acknowledgments**
We would like to thank the following for permission to reproduce photographs: Alamy pp. 13 (© imagebroker), 21 (© Sergio Azenha); Corbis pp. 4, 9 (© Radius Images), 10, 16, 25 (© Ocean), 12 (© Kelly Redinger/Design Pics), 14 (© Denis Balibouse/Reuters), 15 (© Hou Dongtao/XinHua/Xinhua Press), 17 (© Mehau Kulyk/Science Photo Library), 20 (© Andrew Gombert/epa), 22 (© Monty Rakusen/cultura), 23 (© John Madere), 26 (© Dirk Anschütz); Getty p. 5 (Deirdre Rooney/StockFood Creative); Photolibrary pp. 11 (Laura Doss/Fancy), 24 (Kablonk!), 27 (Monty Rakusen/Cultura); shutterstock pp. 6 (© James Steidl), 7 (© Henryk Sadura), 8 (© Dmitriy Shironosov), 18 (© Yuri Arcurs), 19 (© visi.stock).

Cover photo of a worker surveying with theodolite reproduced with permission of Shutterstock (© Dmitry Kalinovsky).

Every effort has been made to contact copyright holders of material reproduced in this book. Any omissions will be rectified in subsequent printings if notice is given to the publisher.

# Contents

Some words are shown in bold, **like this**. You can find out what they mean by looking in the glossary.

# Why Does Math Matter?

Do you enjoy math lessons at school? Do you ever wonder what the point of math is? Math matters because we use it all the time in our everyday lives!

Whenever you buy something you are using math.

Math can be found in unexpected places, such as dividing a cake into slices!

Whatever job you do when you are older, you will need to use math. Some jobs really suit people who enjoy math. Read this book to find out about some great jobs that use math. Could one of them be for you?

# Be a Land Surveyor

If you were a land **surveyor**, it would be your job to measure and record areas of land. You might measure and draw the land before a building project starts. You would make a site plan for **engineers** and builders to follow.

A land surveyor has to check the land before any building work starts.

Land surveyors use tools to measure the land carefully.

Land surveyors have to make sure the land is good to build on. They use many tools and **instruments** to collect information about the land. They use computers to help them make charts and maps of the land they have surveyed.

# Be an Accountant

If you are good with your pocket money, then maybe you could be an accountant! An accountant's job is to look after the **accounts** of a person or company.

Accountants keep track of how much money people are **earning** and spending.

Accountants check how much **tax** a person or company needs to pay to the government. They write reports to show how well a company is doing. They might suggest ways for a company to save money.

Accountants use math in their work all the time.

# Be a Market Researcher

If you were a market researcher, your job would be to collect information. Then you would look at the information and decide how it could help to make things people need. You might do market research for a company that wants to know about its customers.

Market researchers often use math when they put information in a report.

Often, market researchers need to be good at talking and listening to people.

Some market researchers organize surveys to see what people think about something. Other market researchers ask groups of people questions. Then they think about the answers and write a report.

# Be a Structural Engineer

If you were a structural **engineer**, you would help design buildings, bridges, and tunnels. Your job would be to make sure a new structure stays held together.

Sometimes structural engineers check that old buildings are safe for people to use.

Structural engineers often use computers in their work.

Structural engineers have to work with **architects**, builders, and many other people. They need to know a lot about different **materials** and their **properties**. Structural engineers use math to help them design new structures.

# Be a Product Designer

If you were a product designer, you would decide what many of the things people use every day look like. You could design mobile phones or toys. You might help to make new cars or planes.

Some product designers design exciting new vehicles.

Product designers need to make sure the things they design are easy to use and work well. They need to think carefully about who will be using the product and why they need it.

Product designers need to work with careful measurements and use computers to create new ideas.

# Be an Astrophysicist

Do you want to explore the **universe** when you grow up? If you were an astrophysicist, you would study the universe and try to discover new information about it. You might study black holes or learn about stars.

Many astrophysicists teach in universities.

There is still so much to discover about the universe.

Astrophysicists use math as they try to understand the universe. They might use telescopes and other equipment to study the universe. Then they make sense of the information they have found and write about it.

# Be a Financial Advisor

Do you think carefully about how you spend your money? Perhaps you could be a financial advisor. It would be your job to give people advice on how to spend and save their money.

Financial advisors help people spend their money in the best way.

Financial advisors help people to buy houses or save money for when they are older.

Financial advisors think about the best choices for people and explain them carefully. Financial advisors use math every day as they work out what will happen to people's money.

# Be a Software Developer

If you love using computers, then maybe you could be a **software** developer. You would come up with **computer programs** to help people work and play. You might be building computer games or systems that help people to work easily.

Software developers are always looking for new ideas.

Software developers need to think about what the people using the software need. Then they use math to build a test program and test it.

Software developers fix problems with their programs and make the programs work well.

# Be a Data Analyst

If you love working with numbers, then maybe you could be a data analyst. Your job would be to gather information and look at the numbers. You might collect information about how people work, spend money, or enjoy their free time.

Data analysts need to be good at helping others understand how numbers work.

Data analysts use math to understand the information and to present their ideas.

Data analysts decide what the information means and share it with people using graphs, charts, and reports. They might have to **predict** what might happen in the future.

# Be a Math Teacher

If you are crazy about math, then you might like a job sharing this with other people. If you were a math teacher, you would teach students math every day. You could help them to get excited about math, too!

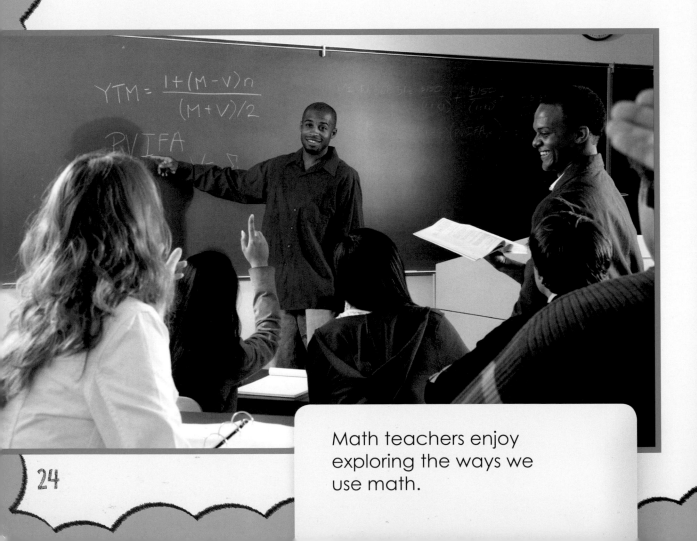

Math teachers enjoy exploring the ways we use math.

Math teachers need to be good at explaining math in a way that students understand. They need to be good at math and enjoy solving puzzles and problems. Teachers need to enjoy working with lots of different people.

Math teachers prepare students to take math tests and exams.

# Choosing the Right Job for You

When you decide what you want to do when you grow up, don't just think about school subjects. Think about what you enjoy doing. If you like working with other people, then you might like to be a teacher or a financial advisor.

If you enjoy working with numbers, then you could be an accountant. If you love space, then think about being an astrophysicist. There are so many exciting jobs that use math that there is something to suit everyone.

## Five things you couldn't do without math

- Spend your pocket money
- Know what time your favorite television program starts
- Share a pizza with your friends
- Measure how tall you are
- Use the index in this book

# Math Job Chart

If you want to find out more about any of the jobs in this book, start here:

| | Accountant | Astrophysicist | Data analyst | Financial advisor | |
|---|---|---|---|---|---|
| **You need to:** | Enjoy using math every day | Be interested in the **universe** | Be good at spotting patterns | Be good at explaining things to people | |
| **Best thing about it:** | Helping people to save money! | Making a discovery that's out of this world! | Seeing your predictions come true! | Helping people to make the right choices! | |

| | Land surveyor | Market researcher | Math teacher | Product designer | Software developer | Structural engineer |
|---|---|---|---|---|---|---|
| | Be good at measuring accurately | Be good at talking to people | Enjoy talking about math | Have lots of ideas | Know a lot about computers | Be good at solving problems |
| | Making sure new buildings are safe! | Finding information nobody has thought of! | Helping pupils understand and get excited about math! | Seeing people use your designs! | Seeing your **software** being used! | Helping to make amazing new buildings that are strong and safe! |

# Glossary

**account**  record of money that has been received or spent

**architect**  person who designs buildings and directs how they are built

**computer program**  instructions that a computer follows to do something

**earn**  receive money for work

**engineer**  person who uses science and math to make tools, buildings, and machines

**instrument**  special tool needed to do a job

**material**  something that is used to make something else

**predict**  say what is going to happen in the future

**property**  how something looks, feels, and behaves

**software**  programs written for a computer

**surveyor**  person who studies the land or a building before construction work

**tax**  money paid to the government

**universe**  everything that exists

# Find Out More

### Math Jobs

www.bls.gov/k12/math.htm

If you're good at math, this Website will give you some ideas for jobs using math and more information about them. If you don't understand some of the information, ask an adult for help.

### NASA

www.nasa.gov/audience/forstudents/k-4/index.html

Check out this Website if you're interested in learning more about space and the universe.

### Smithsonian Education

www.smithsonianeducation.org/students/ideaLabs/universe.html

See how math relationships can help you learn and understand how big the universe and the things in it are at this Smithsonian Website.

# Index